Bill Clanton Books
PO Box 446
Waretown, NJ 08758

Website: billclantonbooks.com
Twitter: @billclantonbiz
Instagram: @billclantonbiz
YouTube: Bill Clanton Biz

Media/Press/Public Speaking Inquiries: 609-891-0072

ISBN: 978-0-9974996-9-8

Garamond font used with permission from Microsoft.
Edited By Julie Shutz

Bill Clanton

Employee to Entrepreneur

Five Days That Changed My Life

By Bill Clanton

Dedication

*Thank you to my wife Natercia for being my best friend
and business partner forever.*

Bill Clanton

Table of Contents

Bill Clanton

Introduction

Before I dive into the documentation of my journey from employee to entrepreneur, I feel it best to tell you a little about myself. I grew up near the beautiful Jersey Shore. I have 2 very supportive parents (Bill and Mary Clanton) that always told me that I could achieve anything I put my mind to. I have one younger sister (Robyn) and one younger brother (Steven). Like most people, I graduated high school, got a part time job, and went to college. For the most part through my early career I did what was perceived as the normal sequence of events. We go to college in the hopes that we'll find both ourselves and the right education that will prepare us for a future career. It is a normal series of events to go to college, get a job, go back to school, get a better job, and keep moving up the ladder.

Prior to college I had a part time job working at a local radio station WJRZ. The station at the time was owned by Mr. Joe Knox. Mr. Knox was kind enough to give a young guy with no experience a job. *Something I'll be forever grateful for.* My dad also worked for the same company as an engineer. However, when I entered college my major was to be a music teacher. I soon realized that this was not my true passion, so I changed my major to Broadcast Journalism. After a few years of community college and working part time an opportunity was presented to me. I was offered a full-time position as a copy writer and production director at the radio station where I already worked part time. I jumped at the opportunity. I was fresh out of college and already had a full-time job in a field that was related to my major, something that is rarely seen in this day and age. By now, I had married a lovely, amazing woman that I met at college and a baby was on the way.

This was when I started to notice that I had a knack for being able to see the big picture. Automation was replacing jobs that were done by radio DJ's for decades. More and more the need for people at radio stations started to decline. From this insight, I took a leap and enrolled myself into a night class at a local trade school. If computers were replacing jobs, I figured that someone had to keep them running. So after about 6 months of night classes and some pretty intense exams I re-entered the job market with a few acronyms after my name. A larger company by this time had purchased WJRZ and I was now working for a larger corporation. It just so happened that the company had an opening in the IT department. So I moved up within the company. After 3 years in the IT department another opportunity was presented to me to head a new department they called "Interactive". This position had me building websites, designing digital assets, editing video and podcasts, for 6 radio stations in NJ. At that time, I truly felt I had arrived! This was an exciting time in my life; I was living the dream, as they say. Well, I did indeed say that for some time, but that was 10 years ago. People change, (insert smug grin here.)

Bill Clanton

Chapter 1

"The Side Hustle Stays on The Side"

How do you define success? This question means something different to everyone. At no time will I push my vision of success on anyone. It helps though to have a vision or mission statement, either written down or in the deep caverns of your mind, which defines what success means to you. Without this it will be very hard to come to grips with what your goals in life are. As you read in the introduction, for me a level of success came in the form of that promotion to head that new department, the "Interactive" dept. For years prior to this I was building web pages and blogs as a hobby, for fun on the side. Now, someone was willing to pay me to do what I considered a hobby or 'side hustle'. I felt that rush of excitement to such an intense degree that I dropped all of my side hustle projects to focus on this new job 100%. This would prove to be a mistake as time went on.

One of my side hustles was the creation of a Pet/Animal blog and streaming radio station called "All Pets Radio". My wife and I had built "All Pets Radio" to be quite successful. People from all over the world were sending us content, product manufacturers were sending us tons of products to review, and we were even receiving a celebrity's welcome at places like the Global Pet Expo. So this is the part where you may want to call me up and yell at me, but I dropped everything, and let "All Pets Radio" die a slow death, so that I could focus on 'the job'. It hurts just writing this now, but mistakes happen for a reason. So we can learn from them. At the time my mentality was not that of an entrepreneur, but of an employee. I put a higher value on having a steady job than I did on perfecting my side hustle. Now, you may ask, "With such a strong love for this job, how did you ever get up the nerve to leave?" Well, the answer to that is simply that sometimes the luster of greener grass can cloud our judgment.

This new job was honestly a fun ride. I was able to stay on the bleeding edge of technology. In fact, it was my job to remain up to date on the latest flashy new gadgets and social networks. It was fun for me, but sheer terror for those that romanticized about radio's glory days. Here I was, the guy coming in and telling everyone that change was on the horizon, and I was laughed at often. Some of my biggest battles were fought during the span of 2008-2011. Not only were many radio executives scared of the shifting audience attention to digital, many remained in denial that radio would ever lose attention.

It was around 2011 that I started to notice a change. This change came in the form of many advertisers seeking out those radio companies that were progressive in the area of internet and digital. One of the reasons the department was started in the first place back in 2007, was that a buy from a major beverage company was lost because of a lack of progressive growth in the digital world. So by 2011, my teaching and development were starting to pay off. I was now being asked to go out on sales calls more often as the account executive's hired gun. I was the guy that could come in to dazzle the client with the "flashy techno babble," as some called it.

You may imagine how this really pumped up my ego. I was "THE GUY" with all the cool and sexy new words and technology. Sad part is, it worked. Nearly every sales call that I was brought in on closed, as a result of my presentations. It was actually quite entertaining to see high level reps from some major brands in fancy conference rooms in NYC playing games that my team had developed for them as a demonstration of our abilities. Or seeing the look on the account executive's face as I whipped out some new bell or whistle that even he didn't know the company had in its arsenal. I can remember one such instance when the buyers around the table were about to get up and leave, their notebooks closed, yet humoring me they asked me if I have anything to add. After my quick presentation we were suddenly all shaking hands, and the account executive was getting signatures. Still to this day, I relish that feeling that I had the power and knowledge to make people listen and close the deal.

This is where things started to change for me. My success with these decision makers gave me so much confidence that I started to question my need for employment. This gave way to my stronger desire for more control and more freedom. At this time, I was not only working this job, but I had rebuilt a few modestly successful side hustles. I was creating mobile apps for a few companies, and I had a few clients that I was developing websites for. So from the outside, it didn't look like I needed to continue working for someone else, but from the inside I still did not feel ready. I did not want to lose my safety net. This, I would think, can be expected of anyone that has a family to support, mortgage, car payments, utilities, etc. Keeping my job was the responsible thing to do, and the side hustle was just play money. Or was it? The only thing MY side hustle was lacking was confidence and time. It didn't require money, with most of what I was doing I was able to continue doing with minimal expenses. However, keeping the day job was what I felt I still had to do.

Before we get too far ahead in the story here, I must also add another piece of the puzzle which also distracted me from the luster of the fancy interactive job. In 2000, I, together with my wife and father, submitted an application with the FCC for an FM license to build a radio station. This was to be a non-commercial radio station.

In late 2007 the FCC finally grated us our construction permit. (Yes it took the FCC 7 years to review our application and grant us the permit.) You'd think that having my own radio station the story would end there, but it didn't. Having the construction permit was only the beginning. The next step was actually building it. June 1ˢᵗ 2010, we officially launched our station. This was possible thanks to the support of family members like my brother Steven, my cousin Galen Baker, and even my Granny Laura Clanton. It was exciting, but at the same time scary because a brand new non-profit radio station meant we all still needed day jobs. I still had to work to pay the bills. I'd work 9-5 for one radio company, and then go home and work all night for my own. Talk about side hustle. LOL

It was a tough struggle, but with some computer automation and a combination of family support we were able to keep things going. The interesting part was that we were able to do all of this without it interfering with our day jobs. It may sound crazy, but even with my own station I still put a higher priority on my 9-5 job. Sometimes we need a wake-up call. Early on in the history of my radio station the wake-up call came in the form of dad having a heart attack only 4 days after the launch of the station. This left me, my wife, my brother, and our close family friend Bob Wick to keep the radio station afloat. We did it, because families pull together when they must. Dad is still with us, and was able to survive his heart attack after a quadruple bypass. By the fall of 2010 dad was back in full steam working at his job as the engineer at the 9-5 job and as part owner and engineer of our station.

Our radio station remained being just a side hustle for both of us. Our 9-5 jobs still seemed to take the higher priority. I still enjoyed the rush of the sales call, the bleeding edge technology, and status of being the go-to, internet marketing "guru" for the company. So on occasion my station would suffer, while I broke my back making sure that account executives at my 9-5 job would succeed. I kept going on sales calls and meetings for a few years, in addition to my regular duties in the interactive department. At one point I was spending more time on the road than in the office. My talents at the bargaining table were in high demand. This also started to wear me down. I'd spend all day on the road with an account executive and then still have to put in another 4-5 hours on other technical issues and work. This lead to the point where this all had to stop, or I needed to be compensated for the extra time. Being a salaried worker meant I got paid the same no matter how many hours I worked. Yet here I was helping account executives put an extra 20-50k in their pockets while I got a pat on the back. I really didn't want much, looking back, I probably would have settled for 3-5% of each sale I helped close. We all know that if we don't speak up, we will never get anything. So that is exactly what I planned to do. I put in for some vacation time, and upon my return I was going to speak up and ask for my percent of the commission.

Chapter 2

"Five Days That Changed My Life"

Before I left for vacation I sent an email to the Regional VP of the company requesting a meeting immediately following my vacation. In my email I explained that I wanted to discuss my future at the company. My initial intention was to request a small part of the commission for every contract that I helped close. I really did not have any plan to quit after my vacation. However, something changed while I was on vacation that changed my life forever. While on my 5-day vacation I decided to pretend for those 5 days that I did not have a job to go back to. This was just my way of having a little fun on my stay-cation. I didn't have big plans to go away, as I'd decided to stay home. So I simply started each day the way I would want to if I were in full control and didn't have the chains of employment. Consequently, what started out as a fun exercise soon turned into a game changing event.

I chose to really define what I could do, and how I could provide for my family. I had many years of experience in the radio field, I had skills with computers, and I knew that I had the knowledge necessary to help others. Still within the confines of my five-day vacation, I started networking with other business owners and simply used my free time to discuss what I could do for them. Remember, I had my own radio station and this was a big part of laying the foundation for my departure. Over the five days I worked from the radio station offices and really tried to get myself into that corporate frame of mind. What happened was more than just a mindset change. Meeting with potential clients and lining up leads became the fuel for my fire. By the 3rd or 4th day it was time for me to have some serious discussions with my wife about taking a leap. As an additional side hustle I had partnered up with a close friend (Tara) to start a small company providing websites and graphic work. But prior to the vacation it had never really gotten off the ground. This vacation afforded me the time necessary to make it a reality. This brought about the birth of WWN Interactive. With the leads I had gathered on my vacation I started to see a growing potential.

Though I am just now mentioning it, in 2010 my wife started a cleaning company. At the time of my vacation in August of 2013 she had already grown her business to where it was bringing in close to half of what my salary was. When we combined the success of my wife's business with the growing potential of my new business, and at the same time still having the side hustle of our own radio station, it was quite obvious that it was time for a big boy decision. We did just that. My wife said something amazing to me and it has stuck with me ever since, "You are not unemployable." Meaning that no matter what the outcome of me quitting my job would be, we would always land on our feet. I was convinced, my wife was convinced, now I just had to convince my mom and dad. I have always put a high value on the approval of my parents. They have always been supportive of me and know that if I set my mind to something I will see it through to reality. I even grabbed the ear of my spiritual mentor Bob Wick, and he too was supportive of the new chapter of my life. So, after several very long conversations with every one that mattered in my life, I knew what I was going to do. I had a meeting scheduled for lunch with the Regional VP of my 9-5 for the Wednesday after my vacation.

Vacation was over and I went back to work with a totally new energy. I was so self-aware and ready for the consequences, good or bad, of the choice I was about to make. The Wednesday lunch meeting started like many previous meetings. We both sat down to lunch at the restaurant, we ordered our food, and after the pleasantries were over I dropped the bomb. "I'm leaving." The look of shock on his face was honestly heartbreaking. I really had a moment there where I heard myself say the words and I almost couldn't believe it, but it was true. I did it, I took the first step towards ending my life as an employee and starting my life as a 100% entrepreneur. This was so scary and yet quite empowering all at the same time. Needless to say, after the initial shock the rest of the lunch was actually quite positive. I knew the Regional VP thought highly of me and supported me, but that became even more evident in the way he supported my decision to leave the company. He of course asked what I would do, and my response was something along the lines of wanting to launch the next Facebook or something very much like that. Without hesitation he nodded and knew that if I said I would do something like that, then I was very well going to do it.

The next 8 weeks were buzzing with me finishing up loose ends and hiring my replacement. The process of hiring was nothing new to me, I had done it many times before when choosing additional staff for my department. This time though I was not just looking for someone that could do the job, I was looking for me. There were several candidates that had enough qualifications to do the work, so the next step was to find someone that would have a personality that would work well with the team. In the end, the process was completed and my replacement was chosen. I agreed to stay on part time for a few weeks while my replacement was being trained. This also gave me enough time to still have a stream of income while I solidified the leads that I set up while on vacation. Finally, on November 1st 2013, I reported for work as an employee for the last time.

Bill Clanton

Chapter 3

"When the Going Gets Tough"

Now free from the confines of my job you'd think that this is where things would be easy. I'm not going to lie to you, this was far from the truth. Now that I was jobless, this is where the work began. Take this into perspective. Being an employee was easy. All I had to do was show up for work and do the list of tasks for the day and go home. The pay check would automatically show up in my bank account. It was someone else's responsibility to get new customers and generate revenue. That was no longer the case for me, I was, for better or worse, in command of my destiny.

This was true. I had several leads for websites and some mobile apps. The moment of awakening then comes as each of those jobs are completed. Not only did I have to complete the jobs, but I also had to be a salesman and get new leads and contracts. Having a partner did help in this area. Both Tara and I worked to get new customers on a regular basis. Early on we were averaging about 2 website projects per month. For our small team of two that was more than enough to keep us busy and fed. This worked out well for us both. My wife was working at her business, I could stay home with my daughter while at the same time bring home my share of the household income. For many of the jobs Tara and I were taking on we didn't stop to evaluate the time cost. We were just so hungry that we would take on whatever job would come our way. This would eventually prove to be catastrophic, at least from my perspective.

We were approached to create a mobile app that was a bit outside the scope of our abilities. However, I was willing to take on the challenge of building a new app that was more complex than anything I had developed prior. This would have been great if it had just been as simple as that. The part that I failed to calculate or estimate was the amount of time this app would really take. The client wanted to create an app that would be on a par with Instagram. Yes, I was so hungry and bold to think that I, one man, was going to recreate an app that took a team of developers to build. Oh, and the catch was I told the client I'd have it done in 8 weeks. 8 WEEKS! If you've ever wondered, I looked it up, it took a year for the first version of Instagram to be released, and then another year of working out the bugs. My client was expecting a fully functional app in 8 weeks. We did not meet the first, second or even third deadlines. The first version of the app made it into production after approximately 14 weeks. As would be expected, it had a fair share of bugs to work out. The client was understanding at first, but eventually not so much.

There were 3 errors made here. I only hope that my embarrassing story may prevent you from making a similar mistake. Error one: I got over confident about my abilities. I learned that it is very important to be self-aware, meaning that we must be aware of our strengths as well as our weaknesses. My over confidence with this project did not allow time for any learning curves, technical delays, or problems. Error two: I did not properly communicate with the client about the amount of time this would really take. In addition, because I was apprehensive when it came to managing the client's expectations, I was reluctant to maintain open communication. Um, DON'T DO THAT! Clients don't like being kept in the dark on projects, and they don't like delays. However, delays are less painful when the client is kept in the loop every step of the way. Error three: We should not have taken this project in the first place. From this event, we learned that just because we are hungry for work it doesn't mean that we must take every job that comes across our desk. We sometimes should be willing to give up the project that costs us too much. Cost is measured in not just dollars. Cost is also a factor of time, stress, and reputation. On a side note, I also under charged for the project. The price was so low that I'm embarrassed to even put it into this chapter.

This major learning experience lasted for about 8 months. After the first version of the app was turning up more and more bugs and errors I came to the conclusion that I would scrap the original app and start over. I spent the next few months developing the 2.0 version, but once again failed to maintain open communication with an already unhappy client. I was determined to make the greatest app ever, but the client wasn't paying for this new version. I took it upon myself to do this, in the hopes of being able to hit the reset button with this client. In the 11th hour, as I was getting the new version ready to send to Apple for approval I was presented with a rather scary certified letter. This letter was filled with lots of legal jargon, but the most important words were CEASE AND DESIST. This was to notify me to stop work on the app and turn over all digital assets for the project to the client. I was more than willing to do so. I packaged it all up, sent it to the client, and I was glad to see this go away. The part that I would never get back was the time I spent working on this app without receiving any payment. DON'T DO THAT.

This turned out to be one of the biggest learning experiences of my entrepreneurial career. The good thing was that this happened early in the process. I figured if I could survive this and keep my confidence up, then I could handle anything. A large amount of this dark chapter in my company's history was painful, but at the same time educational. It truly tested me to see if I had the fortitude to keep going on as an entrepreneur. This helped me to evaluate my own emotional intelligence. I could have let this beat me down. I could have just thrown in the towel, but I didn't.

Rather, I used it as a spring board to better things. I turned the months of development into just time spent getting up to speed on new app building techniques. From that I immediately took on a few mobile app projects that I knew I could handle, and the momentum was growing once again. The lessons I learned in the area of communication brought forth a great awareness of the importance of constant communication with the client. I also got much better at estimating project deadlines and managing the client's expectations. I hope to never have to deal with an episode like this again in the future, but if I do, I know that I will find a way to turn it into something positive.

Chapter 4

"A Little Investment Goes a Long Way"

Even though early on in my new endeavors I was faced with a few mistakes, I didn't let this prevent growth happening within the business. Personal growth is a given. I think that every entrepreneur needs to improve themselves and learn. However, physical practical growth is also necessary. We were hired for several contracts that were fun and encouraging from clients that really appreciated the talents that my partner and I had. Positivity builds more positivity. So, after a few website projects, a few flyers, and a few logo designs we started to realize that it was time for some improvements and investments.

As a business owner or entrepreneur, you should always invest in the product. Investments can take on many different forms. Education is a big method of investing in not only the product but investing in yourself. The great thing about the time we live in is that there are no excuses for not knowing something. Most of my education over the years has come from 2 major sources. (Pay attention here, you may want to bookmark this page for future reference.) GOOGLE and YOUTUBE are your friend. I know that is my own whimsical way of pointing it out, but it is so true. When you are faced with a problem, or you are looking to learn a new skill, the first place to look is Google and then YouTube. For example, as a programmer that was focused on turning out a product as quickly as possible it was easy to do a quick search and then find code snippets that would either give me the pieces I needed, or point me in the right direction. When I made the switch from Final Cut Pro to Adobe Premiere Pro for video editing, I had to get over the learning curve quickly. I sat through many video tutorials on YouTube before I got to a point where I was confident to start using the software. Keep in mind though, this did not cost me anything other than time. Even now, I am still watching videos and learning more and more techniques about Adobe Premiere Pro. The same was true when I decided to try something different and start making coloring books for grown-ups. More on that in chapter 8. As you can see education is just one way you can invest in your business.

Another way of investing in your business is by branding and marketing your business. It is always a chicken or egg scenario when it comes to marketing and advertising. How can you afford to advertise if you don't have customers to pay the bills, and how can you get customers if you don't advertise? Well, I'll tell you now, the latter part of that last statement is the key. You can't have a "field of dreams" mentality when it comes to your business. The competition for most businesses is too intense to just sit back and hope for clients. You must actively market, brand, and advertise your business. I know you may be saying to yourself, aren't those all the same thing? They are related, but each has their own importance as it pertains to investing in your business.

Marketing is the big picture that includes every effort you are making to get your business name known. Marketing may include elements of branding and advertising, but a balanced marketing strategy starts with goals. To put it plainly, a marketing plan is a road map to achieving your goals. For instance, if your plan is to increase your lead count then you need to make that a documented goal. From that point you can develop every other part of your strategy and, as some say, "reverse engineer" a plan to reach that goal. However, nothing should begin until that goal is documented. Next, with the goal of increasing leads, you can now define how you would capture those leads; is it Facebook, is it email, is it phone calls? Finally, you would look to advertise.

Advertising is the method by which people hear about you or hear your message. At a primitive level, taking a bull horn and shouting out your office window is advertising. I don't think it will be that effective, but it fits the formula. That is why knowing where your potential audience is should dictate how and where you advertise. If you find that your audience is on Facebook, then advertise there. If you know that a majority of your customers are AM drive time radio listeners, then bite the bullet and go for it. My lesson here is not to teach you how you should advertise, but more to the point, I want to teach you that you must advertise. Advertising is your fight for your customer's attention.

Branding, as much as it may sound like it goes with marketing and advertising, stands alone. Branding is the method by which customers are able to recognize your name or your company's name and know what it stands for, produces, or is known for. Branding is not so important for a new startup business with no leads, rather branding comes after the reputation is built. Marketing, Sales, Advertising, and Reputation are the actions that lead to branding.

My last suggestion as to how you can invest in your business is exactly what I did next. As you'll remember from earlier, we were always looking for new ways we could serve our clients. One important improvement that was critical to growing our business was that we have the right tools for the job. I remember early on we were doing a photoshoot for a client. We didn't have a professional lighting kit. So, after looking up a few YouTube videos and Pinterest posts we decided to make one. This was quite cheesy, yet effective. It consisted of 2 microphone stands, 2 off the shelf umbrellas, 2 clamp on lights, and lots of duct tape and zip ties. As I said this was effective, but was it presenting the right image for the client? Sometimes the client's impression can make all the difference in the world. The home brew lighting kit was short lived and for a small $150 investment we got a professional portable lighting kit for our offsite photoshoots. Spending a few hundred bucks was not going to hurt the company, and the overall impression of the way we look and conduct ourselves was going to pay us back tenfold. The lighting kit was only one small investment we've made since the start of the company in 2013. Now we are equipped with every piece of graphics, photo or video software available from Adobe, computers, HD cameras of all shapes and sizes, and a plethora of additional gadgets to make us more valuable to our clients. Our latest investment, which we just completed, is our live streaming studio. We are doubling the size of our office space to expand not only the business, but our services as well. I say this not to brag, but to point out that investment and growth are critical for the future success of a business.

Chapter 5

"I'm Free! Or Am I?"

In my post-employee life, I am afforded the luxury of being able to spend more time with my family. However, that doesn't mean that I have time to just goof off; the work still has-to get done. That is where a need for balance comes in. I actually find it amusing that a sizable amount of people think that because I don't punch a time clock I'm on a permanent vacation. (I personally think that way as a positive outlook on my lifestyle, but that is not the perception I like people to have). Being self-employed, or an entrepreneur, does offer me certain freedoms. I can bring my work with me, I can work at odd hours, I can go to my daughter's school in the middle of the day, or I can jump in the car and take the kids to a theme park in the afternoon. I don't have to ask for permission to do any of these things. I'm the boss. This freedom though is a double-edged sword because like I said, the work still has-to get done. Which means that having a balance between work and life should take on a higher priority.

In 2013, when I left my job, my daughter (Caterina) was only one year old, and my son (William III) was 13. I never liked the idea of having my kids spending most of their early years with a babysitter or daycare. For the first 10 years of my son's life my wife was a stay-at-home mom. She was there for him while I was at work. It was not up to a daycare to raise my child for me. My wife only started working again in 2010 when she started her own business. Now with a 1 year old I had to factor my daughter into my grand scheme. I didn't have to give it much thought. I was ready to take on the challenge. So not only was I making the transition from employee to entrepreneur, I was also becoming a stay-at-home, working dad. I had the freedom to do it. My wife in her business she was not able to take our daughter with her, and like I said, it is our responsibility to raise our children, not a daycare. So, the work life balance now had to make room for a toddler.

Working with a toddler in the office brings along with it its own series of comedy and disaster. Some days it was a non-stop request for me or my partner Tara to color with her. Other days it would be blissful as she would get lost in a world of Elmo, Pocoyo, and Winnie the Pooh. There were some funny experiences too. Getting her to eat her lunch was such a challenge, so I would literally remove my belt and anchor her to one of our office chairs to keep her from running around while I tried to get her to eat. By the time she reached two years of age things got a little easier. Having her around also allowed me to realize which clients truly cared about me and not just what I could do for them. If they would tolerate or understand me having my daughter playing on the floor during a meeting I knew we

had something special. For me to do business
with someone they must be willing to hire me and
not just my company. People are what make a
business, not robots. I have some clients now
that are disappointed when my daughter is not
with me. Now that she is five years old and in
Pre-School I have a small window of 'me time' in
the middle of the day for meetings. Many of my
clients that have seen her growing up specifically
look for her to be hanging around my office. My
son over the years has become not only my son,
but also a part of the fabric of my company. He
will often go on photoshoots with me, or get
behind the camera at a video session. Who
knows, maybe one day he'll want to take over this
empire I've been building. I have reached a point
to where I don't apologize for my kids being a
part of my work life. Honestly, it wasn't easy at
first. I mean think about the fact that I was
changing diapers, potty training, struggling
through the terrible twos, battling with a picky
eater, and making time to play while at the same
time building a company, meeting with clients,
building websites, and running a radio station. I
look back and know confidently I would not have
changed a thing. I learned so much through this
whole struggle that now I feel that it has made me
a better father, better husband, and better
entrepreneur. I did on occasion enlist the help of
my extended family to babysit, but I refused to be
dependent on someone else. I also see that some
of what I do rubbed off on my daughter. Her

interpersonal skills in pre-school are exceptional, she is a natural leader during playtime, and she has earned the respect of her classmates. I can't tell for sure if 100% of that is all my doing; I think her strong willed, empowered business owner mommy might have had something to do with that, too. There have been ups and downs, but I love my independence.

Independence is a wonderful thing, and there is no greater feeling than being independent from your employer. But what does employment independence really mean? Rhetorically I ask that question, because most people don't understand the implications that come with employment independence. On the surface, you've already heard me mention the time I get to spend with family and the flexibility of my work schedule. However, there is so much more going on under the hood of this endeavor than that. Self-employment can easily turn into self-enslavement if you are not careful. Managing your time, reducing procrastination, and navigating the ups as well as the downs is what will define you as a business owner or entrepreneur. My freedom from my employer now meant that I alone was responsible for everything. Taxes, healthcare, expenses, sales, marketing, education, travel, and equipment are just a few of the things that you now have to manage. I warn you now, not to discourage you if you had not considered these things. I believe that any one can succeed as a business owner as long as they are willing to put in the work (and time) necessary to make it happen. I only want you to be aware that freedom comes at a cost. But hey, if I could do it, I have no doubt that you can too IF YOU ARE WILLING TO PUT IN THE WORK. As Gary Vaynerchuk says, "Eat $&!% for 24 months, so that you can eat caviar in the 3rd year." Nothing great was ever built without putting in the work. If we back track a little, you'll remember that before I left my job I had already tried several businesses, built a new radio station, and my wife had a successful business. It wasn't that one day I magically wished to be free and poof there it was. When you take into consideration the 5 days that changed my life you can see that the time I spent on vacation was well spent, as I hustled to make my dream a reality. In my case, it just so happened that everything I had done prior to that vacation prepared me for the next step, and the five-day vacation gave me the clarity and organization my dream needed so that I could make employer independence a reality.

Chapter 6

"Life Happens, Or Something Like That"

This may come as a surprise, but nothing lasts forever. When I started my company I had a partner, Tara. She left her job just one month after I left mine. I attribute a large amount of the success of WWN Interactive to her dedication and positive attitude. Working with her was truly a pleasure because we could make up for each other's short comings. What she may have lacked in advanced coding skills she made up for with graphical skills. I had severe procrastination and time management skills, and she was very organized and helped keep me on task. It was a great partnership. Within the company, we would invest 20% of each job back in the company and then split the remaining 80% 50/50. Everything was going great. I was in a groove of managing work load with fatherly duties. The business was growing, and so was Tara's family. Tara and her husband had only been married a year or so, and I knew that eventually this would happen. Tara broke the exciting news to me that she was expecting. I was honestly very happy for her. With my own sister living in another state, I began to see Tara as my sister. So, when she announced that little Zoey was on the way I was thrilled to be an uncle again. Now, let us for a moment take a look at this from the business perspective. What effect will a pregnancy have on the success and growth of a business that is just starting its second year. I must say, Tara was a trooper. Morning and afternoon sickness in the office became accepted routine. Food cravings and all the other trials of pregnancy were now a part of the WWN Interactive circus. When you combine that with the fact that my daughter was now in the terrible twos, it made for some rather hilarious situations.

(Back to the business for a moment) In terms of our business, Tara's pregnancy did not affect our performance or the product we were producing for our clients. It did though leave a big question on the horizon. What would our plan be for after the baby was born? We had nine months to work that out, right? I think that it is important for any business owner, especially when you rely on a partner, to understand that life happens. You can't go into a serious life altering chapter of being a business owner or entrepreneur without having some conscious acknowledgement of life's twists and turns. When Tara and I first started the business, we both knew that a baby would eventually be on the way. We didn't know the specific day, but we knew it would one day be a reality that we would have to face. This left a lot of open questions like; would she work after the baby was born? Would she remain a partner in the company? Would the craving for Costco pizza ever subside? Ok, well the last one may not have been as critical, but it was a question we had to face.

Planning is so important. I know that it is impossible to predict every possible struggle in your business, but some of the basics you can at least have an awareness of. I didn't know exactly when I would be losing my partner, but I had an understanding to expect it. After Tara had the baby she took what would be considered maternity leave. Over this time period, I started looking at the business to see whether now was the time for a change, or would I continue to build this business now on my own?

Tara and I still to this day work together. We just felt it best to allow her the time to be a mommy and just be a freelance graphic designer for me. So, as a result I took over 100% of the company. This had a fair share of benefits and challenges. No longer did I have that other person to share in the stresses, the marketing, and the work. But like I said life happens. I just had to as I usually say, "Put on my big boy pants," and take charge of my destiny. Being self-employed or a business owner means you are the center of all the action. If you are the only person on the team to do the work, then you are the life blood of the business. This means that you don't get a sick day.

I remember several times when I had gotten sick that Tara was there to keep us from falling behind on work. Now, with Tara no longer on the team, there was no such thing as a sick day. I ran into just such a situation in the spring of 2016. As my business evolved I had been taking on consulting jobs that would include designing and installing audio equipment. I was hired by my long time friend Lisa Gallicchio from Preferred Home Health Care and Nursing to travel to the CEO's condo in Boca Raton, FL to install equipment so that he could produce his syndicated radio show from his condo. It was a very exciting gig. I was able to bring the family with me. I only had to work for a few days installing equipment, and then we had a few days for family vacation time. What could possibly go wrong? The day before our departure I started the tell tale signs that something wasn't right. I was coughing heavily; my head was pounding non-stop, and I was practically hitting my inhaler every 5 mins. Now I was about to get on a plane and fly to Florida. I did it. We arrived in Fort Lauderdale, grabbed a rental car, and we were on our way. I was trying every possible home and over the counter remedy to get myself well enough to get the job done. There was no chance of be postponing the trip; I couldn't call out, I couldn't get someone to fill in for me. I had to handle this myself for better or worse. I struggled through it, but in the end, I got the job done. The client was happy. To be honest there were times during this that I wanted to just curl up in a ball and sleep. I mention this simple illustration to show that I am human. Nothing special, just human. The only thing that set me apart was the fact that even though I wanted to give up, I didn't. I put in the work that had to be done and that was it. Remember, nothing great without the work.

The key take away from this chapter, in my opinion, would be that life happens. If you are reading this and hoping to make the leap from employee to entrepreneur you need to understand the hard truth that it is not all glamorous. We do need to get our hands dirty. I think a great way to look at this is to not let our circumstances define us. As Earl Nightingale says in "The Strangest Secret", "A man becomes what he thinks about all day long." If we spend all day thinking about the bad things or difficult circumstances we will only receive struggles. However, if we focus on the positive in every situation we come out as a success. I could have looked at Tara leaving the company as a huge negative, but her departure gave me the push to pursue other areas of the business and to grow personally. I could have looked at being sick as a draw back and let it ruin a great opportunity in Florida. Truth be told, I did find it very tough to think negatively when surrounded by the beauty of Boca Raton. Just look for the positive so that when life happens it doesn't consume you.

Chapter 7

"The Self-Aware Prevail"

The biggest thing you'll need to know more and more about as you grow from employee to entrepreneur is yourself. Self-Awareness must come before you even consider taking the leap. What is self-awareness? Self-awareness is the realization of who you are, what you are capable of doing, and knowing how you will react in any given situation. Some of us start out our working careers while still in high school. Perhaps you take on a part time job or you start flipping things on eBay. At this early age, you are able to see what you like and what you are good at. This extends into our college life, but how many of us actually end up doing what we like vs what we do by just following the herd. It is quite common for us to spend years in college getting a degree for a job we will hate for the rest of our lives. While others that enter the workforce with self-awareness will never work a day in their life because they are happy and excited to do what they love. Self-awareness is what sets them apart. Most people that are successful in life are so because of their ability to look at themselves in the mirror and be real. They know that if they are 5 foot 8 inches they are most likely not going to be an NBA All Star. If they have an uncontrollable fear of heights they are not going to be an airline pilot. You get my point.

It is best that this self-awareness journey start at a younger age only for the simple fact that it is easier for younger people to change lanes on the highway of life. However, it is not impossible for someone in their 40's or 50's or even 60's to make a self-aware change if they are passionate about the end goal. Even now as I write this I'm 40 years old, and I am always fine tuning my plans and goals to pin point exactly what makes me happy, while at the same time makes me money.

You may be saying to yourself, "HOW?" It starts with some basic steps. First, get out of your comfort zone. You'll never be able to find out if there is something better out there if you are constantly living within the confines of your comfort zone. So, experiment, try things you've never done, travel places you've never been, and talk to people that you've never met. Second, read more. Some of the best ways to experience new things is through the eyes of the author. Reading is such a fundamental part of what got me to this point. Read books of fiction, read non-fiction books on topics that interest you, read self-help and motivational books, and also read blogs/articles on topics that interest you. With some consistent focus you are bound to find your next path to follow. Third, don't let fear of failure hold you back. As I mentioned before, you need to experiment and try things you've never tried. Chances are you will fail at your first attempt. It is just a mathematical thing. The more you try the greater your chances for success, but success does not come without a few failures along the way. Fourth, ask the people closest to you what they think your strongest qualities are. You'd be surprise by the way others perceive you. The people who love you the most should know the most about you and what makes you tick, better than you do. Though it is important to keep in mind that not everything you hear will be constructive. The part that makes this constructive is that it is just one of the steps to bringing you closer to being self-ware and ready for the world of entrepreneurship.

I say specifically entrepreneurship and not self-employed. There is a distinct difference between self-enslavement and having the guts and vision to build something bigger than one's self. I use as an example my company when it first started. WWN Interactive on the outside looked and functioned like a big interactive marketing firm. While on the inside it was nothing more than a glorified self-employment operation. Everything in the business was dependent on me or my partner working on every project in order to make money. It can be misleading because of the freedom self-employment offered me. I had the freedom to work where and when ever I wanted, but that didn't make me an entrepreneur. It only took me about a year to fully realize this. Therefore, my next mission was to figure out how to fix it.

In order to be an entrepreneur, I needed to be chasing the potential and not the money. I needed to find ways of investing in projects that would be around for the long term not just a quick buck. As with self-awareness, I had to look deeply into what I was doing and what I could do to make my income sustainable. You'll find that with entrepreneurship not everything is black and white. One day you may make your money building websites, the next day it maybe in affiliate marketing. The options are limitless. In addition, entrepreneurship takes a significant amount of what's called "Delayed Gratification." I imagine that after hearing that you are ready to close the book and walk off, but I encourage you to continue reading, your future depends on it.

Having an understanding of delayed gratification is one of the strongest qualities associated with some of the most successful entrepreneurs. This is the understanding that hard work on a worthwhile goal will be rewarded. Success doesn't happen overnight. Most people that are referred to as 'overnight successes' actually spent years building up to that success. There truly is no such thing as an overnight success, only overnight rewards. Some may refer to this as passive income, and yes, that is one way of looking at it. But, I see it better defined as "Sustainable Income." The income that comes in while you sleep, while you are on vacation, or while you are building your next goal. If you take a good hard look at any successful entrepreneur and closely analyze how they became so successful you will find the same answer every time. They put in the time, did the work, failed, got up from failure, became self-aware, and were content with the delayed gratification. Simply because they set their mind on the goal or prize. They tailored their thinking to visualize what they wanted to achieve, and then they just did it. A successful entrepreneur won't be held back by negative reviews or ridicule from friends and family. A successful entrepreneur has the emotional discipline to pick themselves up. Specifically, because they do not leave themselves vulnerable to any one outside force. One rain storm doesn't not bring down the entire operation. This is because they were able to diversify their streams of revenue.

Diversification is often criticized by those outside the influence of entrepreneurship. Many people have told me to stick to just one thing and not get distracted by others. I tell them that I am only young once, and I'm not going to be the guy that was romantic about shoeing horses. Diversification is the best safety net you can have. However, I'm not encouraging you to over extend yourself to the point of not being able to make anything or any money. Your diverse streams of revenue don't always have to require you doing the work. In fact, it is better when you don't have to. Diversification can come in the form of hiring someone with a unique skill that is currently in demand, it could be starting a mailing list with affiliate marketing strategies, or it could be an entirely different business all-together. My wife in her road to entrepreneurship started with a cleaning company, but has now branched out into event staffing, linen rentals, and even Victorian tea party rentals. Her success is not dependent on the success of any one business, but her sustained stream of revenue is a direct result of her ability to see new opportunities and seize them. I too have reaped the benefits of diversification, and I am still launching new products and services even as I'm writing this now. My wife and I now refer to ourselves serial entrepreneurs. (Not to be confused with cereal entrepreneurs who switch from Cheerios, to Trix, to Capn Crunch!) The key point is that we are happy, doing what we like, and building sustainable streams of revenue.

Chapter 8

"Time To Pursue My Passions"

By the summer of 2015 a new trend was emerging. Honestly, when I first saw it I thought it was a joke. The summer of 2015 was the summer of Adult Coloring Books. This intrigued me to such a point that I had to find a way to get involved. So I launched the website coloringforlife.com to create a place where photos and coloring books could be shared. It wasn't long before I realized that I could create my own coloring books.

In August of 2015 I released my first coloring book for grown-ups called "Colorful Quotes." It was a simple coloring book made of patterns that I created in Adobe Illustrator combined with quotes from some of history's most influential people. By having my first book available through Amazon I earned a bit of credibility in the coloring book world. Authors and Illustrators were now reaching out to me for advice and reviews of their books. That sparked me to create another coloring book, this one being an all hand-drawn Christmas themed coloring book. We can say that I received some of my mother Mary's artistic abilities, so hand drawing this new book seemed to come naturally.

I noticed through this process that it was difficult to find an instruction manual that would tell you how to create a coloring book and then get it published. Once again that light bulb goes off! I decide to document my process of creating my books and publish that as an e-book. It has been 2 years since the coloring book craze kicked off, and I now have 11 coloring books available for sale on the Amazon and Barnes and Noble websites, as well as in several Jersey Shore brick and mortar stores and boutiques.

Growing up I did have an artistic side. I loved drawing and painting, but I never saw a value in pursuing it as a revenue source. By being my own boss I am afforded the time and freedom to explore new ideas or talents that I may have suppressed. When you add together the free time with the confidence to achieve anything I set my mind to, there is no stopping me. Creating a coloring book only had to be done once. Sales will continue indefinitely. Now, every so often, I get a check from Amazon without having to do more work. One might even say that my coloring book empire has become a diversified, passive income for me. Having the coloring books selling on autopilot leaves me even more time to spend digging into other talents, like music.

More than anything in my teenage years my growing passion was music. I played trombone in the school band through high school in just about every band related program that would have me. I won awards, got to perform at some amazing venues, and I loved every minute of it.

I am a self-taught guitarist and still love to play. In college, I had fun writing music and performed occassionally, but I let other people's opinions of musicians get the best of me. This was a time prior to YouTube, so there weren't any outlets for music to get heard other than radio or playing out live. In those next years building a family was a higher priority than my love for music, so as they say, I did not "quit my day job." Honestly, I put my guitar away for about 10 years before I started playing again.

It wasn't until we started attending Grace Calvary Church on Long Beach Island, NJ, that I took my guitar out once again. As we became members of the church, the church elders asked if I had any talents that could serve the church. I remained quiet, but my loving wife spoke up and told them that I played guitar and could sing. I love my wife for that. It just so happened that they had a vacancy in their worship team. I fit right in with the team and soon after became the full-time worship leader. I've been leading worship for 10 years now.

I had been worship leader for a few years before I started writing my own music again. The Pastor even let me introduce songs I had written to the congregation. This was very exciting, so I decided to start recording what I was writing. I had formed a bond with the other guitarist (Jake

Schon) on the team and we formed a band. Incidentally, Tara is Jake's sister. All our families grew to be very close. Jake and I together with Tara and my son William formed a band called "Live Like Him" in 2012.

I know, you may ask yourself, "What does this have to do with entrepreneurship?" It has a great deal to do with it. As a reminder, I left my job on November 1st, 2013. We released our first album December 15th, 2013. This is an accomplishment that would have been pushed back even further if I had a 9-5 job to get in the way. I understand that not everyone can just leave their job and play music all day. The point is that because I put in the hard work and the discipline ahead of time I was afforded the luxury of being able to pursue my passions.

Nothing great happens without putting in the work. I still had to see clients and get work done while we were working on getting the tracks recorded and mastered, but because I worked on my terms I could juggle my schedule in a way that didn't leave me burned out. I remember many times people stopping into my office to see me with a guitar in my hand or sitting at the keyboard working on a song rather than doing the work they expected to see. It started to become a broken record with some of them saying, "It must be nice." And as a matter of fact, yes, it is. (smug grin time) It IS nice because I made it nice. We all

make our own beds. We can CHOOSE to make
the bed with silk sheets or Egyptian cotton just as
easily as CHOOSING to make the bed at all.
Think about it though, doesn't it feel better to
crawl into a nice comfortable neatly made bed
rather than a twisted mess of blankets and sheets?
What did it take to have this luxury? It took a
little work at the start of the day. This holds to
true in business. If you want comfort and luxury
later in the day you need to do the work upfront.
I'm not here to preach about how to manage your
time and work schedule. I only want to share my
experience with the sarcastic short sighted
responses I've received from non-entrepreneurial
minded people. Those are the type that think that
everything I've achieved is by luck or timing.
Those that say, "Well that might work for you,
but I could never do that." Why not? I put in the
work in my day-to-day operation, while still
finding time to work on my music and my
coloring books. Believe me, it is so worth it. My
wife's ambition in building her businesses is
another example of this.

Chapter 9

"The Clean Road To Success"

Around the time we were building the radio station, my wife Natercia started a cleaning company as a way of bringing in extra cash. I was still working my 9-5 job. She started with a $50 clearance model vacuum cleaner, a few rags, and a mop. At first, she started with a partner, but it was obvious that this partner was not in it for the long haul. So my wife took it all on herself to form Natty Cleans and More LLC. She did everything right. The early days of her business started with her working by herself. Her work ethic was amazing, and she put in the hours of work that it took to be a self-employed business owner. The number of clients soon began to grow. Almost all her new clients were coming via word-of-mouth because of the high quality of her work. There was a small amount of traditional advertising done, but the real source of leads and new customers came from word-of-mouth referrals. Referrals are marketing gold. Think about the last time you heard about a new restaurant. Did you go there because of the advertisement? Or was it because your neighbor spoke so highly about how good the food was? I think you see my point here. We, as humans, are more willing to use a product or service after we've heard someone else's review of it. This can happen in one of two ways, positively or negatively.

With most of the clients coming from referrals, my wife quickly learned the importance of having a standard of excellence. What was it that made these people tell others about my wife's company? Anyone can grab a mop and call themselves a cleaning company. My wife's visions for the future included the insight that having return customers was just as important, if not more important, than getting new leads. Return customers are the gears in the referral machine. Happy returning customers in any business are more willing to tell their friends about your business. Natty Cleans has a large number of clients that have been with her for 7 years now. 7 years of satisfied customers has led to exponential growth. This became quite obvious by the 5th year of my wife's business. I had told her all along that if the business could make it to 5 years doubling the number of clients each year, the growth of the 6th year would surpass her greatest expectation. And it did.

With the exponential growth of the company my wife was now able to hire more staff, invest in the company, and plan for her business's future expansion. By having a team of employees to handle more of the work, my wife was free to spend more time on customer service. Because of the high-class status of most of her clientele relationships are critical. As her team focused on getting the work done, Natercia was able spend more time with her clients. The increase in clientele allowed her to invest back into the business by providing things like better equipment and employee uniforms. We both found that doing a few simple things, such as keeping all the employees dressed uniformly, and using high quality cleaning products and tools, really set the right impression. Now each client felt they were getting their money's worth, before the work even began. Obviously, no amount of professionalism can cover up for poor quality of work, but it sure does help set the stage for getting that next referral. My wife was very blessed to have such an elite, high-class clientele. Many of these people were wealthy executives before their retirement or had founded successful companies that are still thriving today. This gave my wife a unique opportunity to learn. With the extra time to build relationships she could talk to these successful people and learn about their story. A simple day at work for her is like visiting her own mastermind team of successful entrepreneurs to bounce ideas off and much more. Quite often it's from these conversations that amazing ideas will surface for the future expansion of her business.

This is where my wife transitions from being a self-employed business owner to being an entrepreneur. If you remember earlier in the book I said that entrepreneurs focus on the potential, and that is exactly what my wife did. From some of her "mastermind" discussions she developed 2 ideas. The first was to offer linen rentals. We live in a transient vacation spot with many vacation rental homes. Home owners and real estate agents were already contracting Natty Cleans to do what's called "change over" cleanings as one set of renters are leaving and the next are moving in for their weekly rental. Sheets and towels are almost never supplied with these rentals. Therefore, the renter needs to bring these items with them or purchase them. Seeing the potential in providing this service I jumped on board and "LBI Linens" was born.

When you reach a point where your primary business can make money as if on autopilot, it provides an opportunity for developing new products and services. From the cleaning revenue, we were able to invest in new ventures. The linen company is still in its infancy. Still, we are already starting to see potential for a significant return on investment.

The second idea that my wife was able to formulate from her "mastermind" discussions as I call them, was "Tea Party to Go." My wife had a modest collection of Victorian china teapots and tea cups. Several of her clients had asked to borrow her collection for tea parties at their homes. The "ah ha" moment struck and we both said why not get paid for letting someone use the collection. This project is still in development, we haven't even built a website for it yet, but we already have tea parties booked.

My wife has done an outstanding job of building an empire, and she is nowhere near done. At the time of writing this we are looking for a building. For the past 7 years, she has pretty much run her business out of her van. With the significant growth of the business a building has become a necessity. In addition, we are also putting together a fleet of branded vehicles. Oddly enough after 7 years of running a successful business there are still people, friends, and even family that don't take the business seriously and don't see it as a "real" business. I find myself mentally screaming, "Um, HELLO, the business brings in 3 times my old salary!", but people judge based on traditional success measures. With the acquisition of a building Natercia will not only be able to work more efficiently to serve her clientele, she can change the perception of the business. Incidentally, my wife has on occasion gotten calls from other cleaning companies asking for advice on how they should run their company. This new building will give Natercia a place to expand even further to develop a consulting program and training course.

Please be mindful, this success took work to get here. I joke about this all the time, but it is quite true. My wife had to clean a lot of toilets before she reached this level of success. Nothing great comes without putting in the work, and in my wife's case, the quality of the work is critical. I could go into more detail talking about her journey, but that will be left for another book.

Chapter 10

"Reputation Cannot Be Bought"

What was it that made people want to tell their friends and family about my wife's cleaning company? With so many other cleaning companies available why did they refer hers? It comes down to just one word, reputation. The "clean" reputation of her work and her cleaning company in some cases actually presented her with both positive and negative results. Many were quick to boast about her service and refer her. Others loved her service so much that they didn't want to risk losing her or didn't want to share her. Think about that for a moment. She had client's that loved her so much that they didn't want to share her. That is very powerful. That's what I call customer satisfaction.

I'm inferring by now that if you've read this far, you are either interested in building a business or improving your existing business. Let's apply this thinking to your own business. High quality services and work pave the way to improving your reputation. Reputation though, is comprised of more than just doing a good job. My wife was exceptional at always leaving the clients' homes better than she found them, and her 'level of quality' or 'standard of excellence' extended beyond that. Many of my wife's clients and even many of my radio and web design clients now feel such a level of trust in our services that they will buy from us forever. Our reputation for providing quality service while being reliable has afforded us certain luxuries. Luxuries in the form of referrals and repeat business of course, but also in the form of what I call "self-service clients." My wife has seen this the most frequently with her business. She has some clients that she obtained through referrals from other satisfied customers. The positive perceptions of these new clients were based entirely on the praise of their trusted friends and/or associates. This is a common scenario. Natercia will receive a call or text message from a potential client, after a quick exchange of the usual info like size of the house, total rooms, and the address she'll have the deal closed. The client will then either leave her the key or mail her the key. Through this entire process, she will never actually meet the client in person. She may go weeks cleaning this home and never have any interaction with the client other than small talk or via the invoice and check. If the quality of the work meets the expectations of the client the relationship runs on autopilot.

How did this come about? New clients without even meeting them? Autopilot business? It all comes back to the reputation. Not just the reputation of my wife's business, but also the integrity of the person doing the referring. Your reputation is your best weapon when battling with your competition. My wife has a fair share of competition. Other companies spend large budgets on advertisements, they have a bigger staff, and several have huge fleets of branded vehicles. Shouldn't that be enough to force her out of the marketplace? Well truth be told, no, and in many cases my wife is usually the one brought in to save the day after other cleaning companies fail. I don't say this to brag or boast, I am simply stating fact based on actual surveys and discussions with clients. In each case the other companies lost the sale because they failed to provide a consistent level of quality, thus tarnishing the reputation of the business and not getting the referral.

From an entrepreneur's perspective, it is much easier to sell to an existing customer that you have a relationship with than to work on getting new leads and having to start from scratch each time. So, doesn't it make more sense to focus on quality work, nurturing relationships and the bigger picture? It is the age-old marketing struggle of quantity over quality. Perhaps for a self-employed person chasing the money, quantity seems more enticing. It should be easily recognized that it is the entrepreneur that can chase the potential, focus on quality, and embrace the delayed gratification that will win at the end of the day.

The entrepreneurial perspective on reputation and potential can, from the outside, seem to move slowly. Again, nothing great has ever happened without putting in the work. Over time, my wife and I have learned that when you take control of the speed that your business operates, you can be more selective. You can decide how many clients you take on, or if you want to take a specific project or job, and in the end, you get to evaluate if each new client will hurt or help your business. When you take your mind off chasing money, you can evaluate each step along the way and how it will impact your reputation. Taking on a high maintenance client just to get the quick cash can be counterproductive. Together we have observed that when you count the hours spent trying to please the unpleasable, it becomes self-evident that in far less time you could have gotten 4 or 5 new clients.

I mentioned earlier in the book that just because you CAN do it, doesn't mean you SHOULD do it. Well, the same thing holds true in that you shouldn't be afraid to fire the client. If you have a client that is either holding you back, interfering with your day to day business beyond the scope of their contract, and in some cases causing potential risk to your reputation, FIRE THEM. Make certain that when you sign a contract with a new prospect you leave yourself and your client a way out.

On a similar note your work load can hurt you. Taking on too many jobs without enough staff to provide the same level of quality that your customers expect can also hurt you. It may sound contrary to what your accountant would want to see as far as the bottom line, but in the long run you'll be pleased with yourself for doing it. All for the simple reason of keeping your reputation, as in my wife's case, "squeaky clean." But all kidding aside, this topic of reputation comes up almost daily in our entrepreneurial world. Your reputation should be something you put above all else. No amount of money can buy a good reputation, why would you ever put that in jeopardy.

With a modest amount of effort any business can achieve the value packed referrals that my wife has received with her business. Though there is one referral based topic that I failed to mention thus far. Paid or incentivized referrals. Up to this point every referral that I've spoken of has been non-compulsory. In other words, she did not offer any special discounts or bonuses for these satisfied customers to refer her. I'm sure we've all seen it or remember the commercials, "tell your 10 friends and family and get the free phone." However, when your reputation and quality of work speak for themselves you don't need to "buy" your referrals. Now, she has given select clients a discount after receiving referrals, but the incentive was not used as bait for referrals. As you may have noticed, I am very proud of my wife for what she has achieved, and for what we've achieved together. Neither one of us went to business school. We didn't have entrepreneurial families either.

Through our mistakes and successes, we've been able to develop our own "common sense" theory of how to run a successful business. Now we are able to treat all future ventures with the same attitude, giving ourselves a greater chance of success because we've already put in a majority of the work.

Bill Clanton

Chapter 11

"4500 Watts of Pure Potential"

With everything else I was building between my coloring book empire, my music, my wife's business, and my interactive web design company, I still had a radio station to run. My radio station is a non-profit radio station, but just like commercial broadcasting companies we share the same struggles that any business faces. Bills still need to get paid in order for there to be a product to market. As I stated at the beginning of this book, just 4 days after the launch of the radio station my father suffered a heart attack. This did have an effect on the entire family running the station, but it also helped me grow a little. My father's near death experience reminded me of a few things, but most importantly that I wasn't always going to have Dad around to run to when things went wrong. Dad is still with us, and I cherish the fact that I have a partner in the business for support, but being able to put on the "big boy" pants and take command of the company was also necessary.

Running a radio station is not all that different from running any business. The only major point of difference is the 4500 Watt signal that reaches a wide audience with minimal advertising. Over these 7 years on the air we have been able to cater to our local audience and provide music and content that people claim to personally possess as 'theirs." Many will say "My music" or "My Radio Station" in their description of the station. This is another example of reputation and quality product. We didn't launch this radio station without a fair amount research into what format we would go with. At the start of my radio career I had the privilege of producing a show on local radio station WYRS in Manahawkin NJ. This show became the testing ground for what would eventually become WBNJ in Barnegat NJ. I was on the air at WYRS for almost 20 years before WBNJ even saw the light of day. I knew from my years of experience what music was going to capture the audience and leave them wanting more. So, by offering a quality product that my audience takes ownership of, I can benefit from some serious word of mouth advertising. Listeners are more than happy to share with their friends and family what they have found on our air waves. This can be related to any product or service. If you do your research and provide a quality product that your audience can get emotional about, they will do the advertising for you.

Because we are the media company for our own brand, we are able to sell sponsorships on the radio station. This is how we make money, and keep the lights on. If you truly analyze what I've done here, building a radio station by today's standards is almost a step backwards. We are in a day and age where traditional media like radio, television and newspapers are losing audience. Why on earth would I put so much effort into a dying medium? Well, I never lost faith in radio and I never will. In my employed life working for a large radio company I faced many struggles getting the traditionalists to see the value in the web products. My battle cry was always "Does it suddenly stop being radio just because someone consumes it on their computer or phone rather than their car radio?" I still hold true to that today, and I've found ways of merging the traditional with the innovative, by growing our distribution and repurposing of content. We produce local talk programming which in turn becomes 4 different podcast feeds. With tools like Facebook live we capture the momentum and excitement of main street and bring it to our audience where ever they may be. A video on Facebook at local events becomes soundbites to be used on the air, or full length audio captured becomes podcasts. We focus more on the content creation and less on being romantic about the method by which people consume it. Having the license and the antennas gives us street credibility for the traditionalists and our digital efforts keep us relevant with an ever-evolving audience.

In addition to growing technologically we have also grown in other ways. When we first launched the radio station, our studios were in my home office. This was fine for the first year, but as our staff grew and our capabilities grew we needed to expand. We found a great office location in a very visible building on main street with great signage. We struggled to keep the bills paid, but it was necessary for the growth of the radio station. We are still in that same building today. We have since expanded to include not only our unit, but also the 1000 square foot unit next to ours, which now houses our interactive video and production studios. Other growing pains included the addition of new staff members and building a team that shared my vision for the radio station. I had no problem working my butt off building this station into the product it is today. However, just like any business, as it grows you soon realize that you can't do everything yourself. As you may know already, getting people to share your dream and passion is often a struggle, so in this case I've cherry picked my staff to only include people who are as passionate, if not more so, than me about the radio station and its mission. I think that being very particular with who you allow on your team is what can make or break a business. The people who are closest to you in your business structure should share your passion or at least take pride in having a common goal of the success of the business. I've truly been blessed in this area. I've surrounded myself with people that I've worked with for many years that I trust, and they also trust me. This too is critical, a leader needs to have the trust of his followers. I may not be perfect in running every aspect of this radio company, but I know my team won't let me down.

Having come from working for a radio company that is literally down the street from my office, and having my dad still employed by that same company there is certainly opportunities for some awkwardness. When I left my previous job, I made it a point to not burn any bridges. I am willing to "play nice in the sandbox" whenever our 2 companies are involved with community events. I've even come to my previous employer's rescue when lightning had struck one of their facilities. We as business owners cannot afford to allow petty nonsense to hurt relationships. This is what business owners need to do. We need to sometimes put aside our differences and focus on the greater good of building a better marketplace for all businesses.

Chapter 12

"Be Courageous Following Your Mentors"

Every entrepreneur needs a mentor. I have followed many different motivational speakers over the years including John Maxwell, Brian Tracy, Tony Robbins and even the late Charles "Tremendous" Jones. Through their books and their speeches, I've been able to take the words they teach and let it shape and guide my entrepreneurial spirit. Having the discipline of self-education, I feel, is at the heart of every successful entrepreneur. We should never stop learning. In addition, I've followed practical business motivators such as Gary Vaynerchuk. Gary's story and real world advice on business and the behavior of the market has given me have the confidence to engage with the intuition in my heart. The first time I heard Gary speak I was immediate encouraged by the fact that finally I had found someone that thinks the way I do. It is a known fact that if you don't put in the work to build your dream, you'll spend the rest of your life helping someone else build theirs. Mentors not only educate entrepreneurs, but they provide encouragement along the way. This is for me comes also in the form of admiration for some more local less nationally known entrepreneurs.

As I was finalizing my outline and notes for this last chapter, I had the opportunity to speak with an entrepreneur that I've had the pleasure of working for, but also someone I consider a friend.

Joel Markel is the founder and CEO of Preferred Home Health Care and Nursing. Joel was kind enough to allow me to ask a few questions about his views on entrepreneurship. Here are some highlights from our discussion and some powerful bullet points.

Q: What makes entrepreneurs different than most people in the workforce?

Joel: *As an entrepreneur you want to prove to yourself that you can be bigger than your circumstances. An entrepreneurial spirit is one that wants to get up and try new things when the reality of life is pulling you down.*

Q: Many will say that successful entrepreneurs just got lucky, what is your take on that?

Joel: *You can't just show up and expect success. You need to be the landlord of your own existence. You need to put in the effort.*

Q: Do you think that entrepreneurship is something that can be learned or is it something we are born with?

Joel: *Entrepreneurship can be learned, if you have the drive put in the work.*

Q: How do you find innovative ways of growing your business?

Joel: *Surround yourself with talented people that can bring new options and innovations to you.*

Q: If you could pass one piece of advice to your younger self in the past what would that be?

Joel: *Do what your heart is telling you sooner and be courageous.*

That last statement from Joel is probably the biggest piece of advice that stuck with me after our discussion. "Do what your heart is telling you sooner and be courageous." We can't get wrapped up in our fear of failure. Forget everyone else's opinions and prove to yourself that you can do it. You CAN rise above and pick yourself up! It simply comes down to practical application of the knowledge that these motivators teach. In this current state of media and internet, there really can be no excuse for not improving your outlook on success. If you can't afford to see these speakers live, then buy their books, if you can't buy their books then watch their videos on YouTube, if that's not enough listen to podcasts. Many entrepreneurs like myself want nothing more than to see you succeed. Every one of us has a different story as to how we got here. What worked for me may not work for you. However, you'll truly never know until you try. When I took that five day vacation, and started to map out my future, the fear of failure seemed to vanish. My determination was my fuel. Using the years of motivation and mentorship I had received both in books and in person prepared me to make a decision. Now I look back and chuckle thinking that all it took was five days of pretending that I was an entrepreneur to push me over the edge to becoming one. Years of education and experience set ablaze by an almost childish game I played by myself. Becoming the one thing that I thought about for so long.

In August of 2013 I took a vacation that would become the *five days that changed my life*.

Bill Clanton Books
PO Box 446
Waretown, NJ 08758

Website: billclantonbooks.com
Twitter: @billclantonbiz
Instagram: @billclantonbiz
YouTube: Bill Clanton Biz

Media/Press/Public Speaking Inquiries: 609-891-0072

ISBN: 978-0-9974996-9-8

Garamond font used with permission from Microsoft.
Edited By Julie Shutz

Stay up-to-date with all of Bill's projects by
visiting billclantonbiz.com

www.ingramcontent.com/pod-product-compliance
Lightning Source LLC
Chambersburg PA
CBHW031603040426
42452CB00006B/398